Spitfire Faces

Spitfire Faces

The Men and Women
Behind the Iconic Fighter

Dilip Sarkar Sarkar MBE, FRHistS

AIR WORLD

First published in Great Britain in 2023 by
Pen & Sword Air World
An imprint of
Pen & Sword Books Ltd
Yorkshire – Philadelphia

ISBN 978 1 39906 531 3

A CIP catalogue record for this book is
available from the British Library.

Typeset by Mac Style
Printed in the UK by CPI Group (UK) Ltd, Croydon, CR0 4YY.

Pen & Sword Books Limited incorporates the imprints of Atlas, Archaeology,
Aviation, Discovery, Family History, Fiction, History, Maritime, Military, Military
Classics, Politics, Select, Transport, True Crime, Air World, Frontline Publishing,
Leo Cooper, Remember When, Seaforth Publishing, The Praetorian Press,
Wharncliffe Local History, Wharncliffe Transport, Wharncliffe True Crime
and White Owl.

For a complete list of Pen & Sword titles please contact

PEN & SWORD BOOKS LIMITED
47 Church Street, Barnsley, South Yorkshire, S70 2AS, England
E-mail: enquiries@pen-and-sword.co.uk
Website: www.pen-and-sword.co.uk

Or

PEN AND SWORD BOOKS
1950 Lawrence Rd, Havertown, PA 19083, USA
E-mail: Uspen-and-sword@casematepublishers.com
Website: www.penandswordbooks.com

Contents

Introduction

Paradoxically, whilst disarmament and a lack of government spending on defence held sway between the wars, a period aptly described by Churchill as the 'years of the locust', it was, nonetheless, an exciting time for aviation – towards the end of which, just in the nick of time, the Supermarine Spitfire first flew. That the little fighter designed and built on the banks of the river Itchen near Southampton went on to become, and remains, *the* icon of British national pride nearly a century later, would doubtless surprise its creator, the genius Reginal Joseph Mitchell, who tragically died, prematurely, of cancer even before the Second World War erupted. Mitchell was never fully aware, therefore, of his essential contribution's enormity – which went on, incredibly, to be developed, overseen by unsung-hero Joe Smith, through twenty-four marques and ultimately enjoying performance unimaginable back in 1936.

Intended as a short-range defensive interceptor, the Spitfire's advantage during the early war period over its stable mate, the then more numerous Hawker Hurricane, was its superior high-altitude performance. This meant that Mitchell's fighter – and Mitchell's fighter alone – was able to reach the high-flying Me 109s, providing a protective umbrella below which the Hurricanes could go to work against enemy bombers at altitudes it was better suited to. Make no mistake, without that high-altitude capacity, the Battle of Britain's outcome could have been very different – which is the logical conclusion of studying evidence, and not blindly subscribing to a myth.

By the spring of 1941, the Spitfire was completely replacing the Hurricane as the RAF's frontline fighter, and so the arms race went on, with the Me 109, which initially enjoyed certain technical advantages over the Spitfire, continuing to improve, with the Spitfire having to keep up – until Kurt Tank's Focke-Wulf 190 appeared on the Channel coast in the autumn of 1941, which, in the words of the RAF's official top-scoring fighter pilot, Air Vice-Marshal Johnnie Johnson, 'saw everyone off and drove us back to the French coast'. It would not be until the following year that the Spitfire Mk IX, with its two-stage supercharged Merlin engine providing terrific boost and performance, 'returned', as Squadron Leader Danny Browne, an American serving in Johnnie's Canadian Wing at Kenley remarked, 'the air to us'.

As the Second World War progressed, the air war evolved and changed. In North Africa the Desert Air Force learned and perfected the art of tactical air support, which was honed further still during the invasions of Sicily and Italy. Then, of course, came D-Day, on 6 June 1944, when Allied troops, at last, landed in Normandy – beginning the 'Long Trek' across Europe into Germany itself. With the Luftwaffe so heavily committed defending the Reich against American bombers by day and RAF Bomber Command by night, the RAF fighter pilots' role became more about tactical air operations, dive-bombing and strafing enemy troop movements and strongpoints, supporting the advancing Allied armies. In the Far East too, the Spitfire played its part against the Japanese, so the Spitfire became a familiar shape in the skies of every theatre of operations, even flying from aircraft carriers as the 'Seafire', and high-altitude, unarmed, photographic reconnaissance missions – things certainly never envisaged by R.J. Mitchell.

The design, technical and operational history of the Spitfire has been written many times, the iconic fighter enjoying a burgeoning bibliography which, incredibly, continues expanding even today. Over 22,000 Spitfires were built, so just how many people, over the years, were somehow involved with the aircraft in some way, is impossible to say – but runs into many hundreds of thousands. This book, though, is not intended to be yet another history of the Spitfire – but it is about Spitfire *people*. That said, it is neither an attempt to provide a comprehensive photographic overview of all the different roles that made, maintained and operated the Spitfire, although it does in part. My personal interest is mainly in the fighter air war over north-west Europe, and the photographs presented here are images donated to or somehow absorbed into my archive over many years. Most are unauthorised amateur snapshots, taken at a time when photography on service installations was prohibited for security reasons – that alone making them remarkable. Others are official photographs. Every picture, as they say, tells a story. As with certain of my other titles, not least the recent and comparable 'Faces of The Few', there could well be other volumes sharing more photographs. From a young age I understood the importance of collating these images with a view to one day making them widely available and with context – so here you have it: 'Spitfire Faces', a unique collection of photographs of some of those wonderful people who designed, built, maintained and flew the incomparable, *Spitfire*!

Dilip Sarkar MBE FRHistS, 2022

Reginal Joseph Mitchell became the Chief Engineer and Chief Designer at the Supermarine Company, Woolston, in 1920, and his place in history is assured as one of the most gifted aircraft designers of all time. Mitchell's creations included the Schneider Trophy winning seaplane racers, the experience of designing which led directly to the Spitfire fighter.

The Spitfire prototype, K5054, made its maiden flight from Eastleigh on 5 March 1936, at the hands of test pilot, Captain J. 'Mutt' Summers (extreme left), pictured on that very day with R.J. Mitchell (seated), and others involved with producing the new fighter, namely from left: Major Harold Payn (Assistant Chief Designer), Mr S. Scott-Hall (Air Ministry Resident Technical Officer), and Jeffrey Quill, later to become Supermarine's Chief Test Pilot.

The only photograph ever taken of R.J. Mitchell with his Spitfire, namely K5054, shortly after the first flight at Eastleigh, this snap taken by his son, Gordon. Tragically, Mitchell died on 11 June 1937, aged 42, so did not live to appreciate the immeasurable contribution he had made to preserving the western democracies by creating the Spitfire.

Gordon Mitchell, photographed by his father with K5054 at Eastleigh in March 1936.

Dr Gordon Mitchell was, understandably, incredibly proud of his father's achievements and wrote his own history of 'R.J.'s time at Supermarine (see bibliography). Indeed, Gordon spent his retirement campaigning to see his father honoured posthumously for designing the Spitfire, but as the honours system fails to provide for posthumous awards, this never happened. Gordon died in 2009, aged 88.

Joe Smith was Supermarine's Chief Draughtsman when the Spitfire was designed, and after R.J. Mitchell's death he oversaw the production and development of the aircraft. Whilst the credit for creating the Spitfire belongs to Mitchell, it is to Joe Smith that the honours should go for having worked on developing the Spitfire through its many years of operational service.

Supermarine employed many local people, including Cyril Russell, of Bitterne, Southampton, who began work there aged 16 as a sheet metal apprentice, remaining with the company until 1957. His autobiographical account *Spitfire Odyssey* remains essential reading (see bibliography).

Supermarine's Research Department was based at Hursley Park, between Romsey and Winchester, this being Marjorie Oliver and Harry Griffiths pictured there in 1942. (via Dave Key and 'The Supermariners')

Marjorie Oliver pictured in the research laboratory at Hursley Park. (via Dave Key and 'The Supermariners')

The Supermarine Research Department at Hursley Park, 1942. (via Dave Key and 'The Supermariners')

The contribution of females to the Spitfire story must not be overlooked: this is Bunty MacCallum, a tracer in Supermarine's Drawing Office, who married George Wherley, one of the draughtsmen. (via Dave Key and 'The Supermariners')

On 4 August 1938, Supermarine Chief Test Pilot Jeffrey Quill delivered the RAF's first Spitfire to 19 Squadron at Duxford. During the subsequent Battle of Britain, Quill insisted upon flying Spitfires with 65 Squadron at Hornchurch, to gain experience of the aircraft in combat conditions. He is pictured here having delivered Spitfire AB910 to the RAF Historic Aircraft Flight at RAF Coltishall post-war; 'J.K.Q.' died in 1996 after a lifetime in aviation.

When 19 Squadron received that first Spitfire, the unit was commanded by Squadron Leader Henry Iliffe Cozens, AFC, to whom the credit goes for introducing the Spitfire to operational service without losing a single man.

In 1985, Air Commodore Cozens (left) was reunited at Duxford with Jeffrey Quill (in cockpit) and Wing Commander Pingo Lester, who was Station Commander at Duxford when that first Spitfire, K9789, was delivered by Quill on 4 August 1938.

Some of the very first Spitfire pilots on 19 Squadron at Duxford, from left: Pilot Officers 'Ace' Pace and Ian Robinson, Flight Lieutenant Wilf Clouston, Flying Officer Arthur Banham and Pilot Officer Eric Ball; seated is Flying Officer Eric 'Tommy' Thomas.

The Spitfire was designed and intended as a short-range daylight interceptor; with its narrow-track undercarriage and glowing rows of exhausts either side of and in front of the pilot, it was not suited to night-flying. On 21 December 1939, 19 Squadron's Pilot Officer Horace Trenchard was killed in Spitfire K9809 during a night-flying accident in which the pilot, having only just taken off, became disorientated and dived straight into the ground. The New Zealander was buried at nearby Whittlesford, a long way from his Wellington home.

Having been preserved for home defence, so desperate was the hour that in May 1940 the Spitfire squadrons were deployed to provide aerial cover for the Dunkirk evacuation. To increase range, the Spitfires congregated at airfields in the south-east, and met the Me 109 over the French coast for the first time. These are armourers of 19 Squadron at Hornchurch, from which station the unit operated during DYNAMO.

Three other 19 Squadron pilots who saw action over Dunkirk. From the left they are: Sergeant Jack Potter, later captured during the Battle of Britain; Flying Officer Geoffrey Matheson, ultimately reported missing flying Mosquitos; and Pilot Officer Peter Watson, shot down and killed on the Squadron's first full-formation combat, on the morning of 26 May 1940.

Pilot Officer Michael Lyne was wounded when his Spitfire was shot-up over the French coast on 19 Squadron's second full-formation operation on 26 May 1940, crash-landing on Walmer Beach and as a result of which he missed the forthcoming Battle of Britain. A Cranwellian, Michael went on to enjoy a stellar service career, retiring from the post-war service as an air vice-marshal; he died in 1997.

Flying Officer Richard Hellyer was a founding member of 616 'South Yorkshire' Squadron of the Auxiliary Air Force, which received Spitfires in October 1939. He recorded combat successes over Dunkirk and survived the mauling 616 received at Kenley in August and September 1940. He died in 1995.

Flying Officer Edward 'Teddy' St Aubyn, a former Grenadier Guards officer turned auxiliary airman at Leconfield after a night-time mishap involving this and another Spitfire, which can be seen in the distance. St Aubyn survived being wounded in the Battle of Britain only to be reported missing whilst flying army cooperation Mustangs in 1943.

RAF expansion before the Second World War led to the regular and auxiliary air forces being reinforced by trained pilots from the RAF Volunteer Reserve, young men who remained in their civilian occupations, learning to fly at weekends, and who were available for mobilisation in the event of a crisis. This is one such reservist, Sergeant Patrick Sherlock Hayes, a bank clerk, who joined the VR in 1937. On 7 July 1940, he was flying Spitfires with 65 Squadron at Hornchurch but was reported missing following combat with Me 109s over the Channel. As the Battle of Britain did not officially begin until three days later, his name will not be found amongst The Few – his story is told in the author's *Battle of Britain 1940: The Finest Hour's Human Cost* (2020).

Another fighter squadron to see action over Dunkirk and be heavily engaged throughout the Battle of Britain was 74 'Tiger' Squadron, the groundcrew of which are seen here with a Spitfire Mk IA at Biggin Hill in 1940.

A famous 'Tiger', Manston, spring 1941: Flight Lieutenant John Freeborn DFC of 74 Squadron, an ace of the Battle of Britain who survived the war and died peacefully.

'Tigers' at Gravesend, 1941; from left: Pilot Officer Bob Poulton, Flight Lieutenant John Freeborn DFC, Squadron Leader Baker, Flying Officer Woods, and Pilot Officer Tony Mould. The Spitfire, an Mk IIA, P8388, 'Black Vanities', was a presentation aircraft (more of which later) presented by the Black family of London Palladium fame.

From the personal album of 74 Squadron's Bob Poulton, an excellent snapshot of a 'Tiger' sergeant-pilot with a Spitfire Mk IA, circa 1940, starter trolley accumulator plugged in, ready to go – but who is he?

This appears to be the same 74 Squadron sergeant-pilot, again from Bob Poulton's album – a good study of a pilot at readiness.

Another unidentified 74 Squadron pilot from Bob Poulton's album, circa 1940. Despite the cold at altitude, the Irvin sheepskin flying jackets were unpopular in the air with Spitfire pilots owing to being too bulky in the aircraft's cramped cockpit.

Another unnamed pilot in Bob Poulton's album, but known to be Flight Lieutenant W.J. Sandman, a New Zealander of 74 Squadron, who was shot down over France in Spitfire Mk VB W3120 on 27 June 1941, and captured. This Spitfire, pictured at Manston in April 1941, is a Mk IIA, P8261, ZP-N, and bears the 'sky' day-fighter band around the rear fuselage.

Yet another unidentified Spitfire face from Bob Poulton's album, this being a Flying Officer of 92 Squadron snapped at Biggin Hill in late 1940.

Air Commodore Herbert 'Tubby' Mermagen (centre) was a pre-war Cranwellian, a gifted aerobatic pilot and flying instructor. He saw action over Dunkirk and during the Battle of Britain whilst commanding 222 Squadron, and survived the war to enjoy a long career in the service. Pictured here (centre) with a Tempest aircraft post-war, this keen golfer retired to Painswick, Gloucestershire, and died in 1998.

A member of 222 Squadron's groundcrew in the cockpit of P9323, ZD-F, at Hornchurch during the Battle of Britain. This Spitfire Mk IA was shot down and abandoned by Sergeant Spears over the Isle of Sheppey on 31 August 1940.

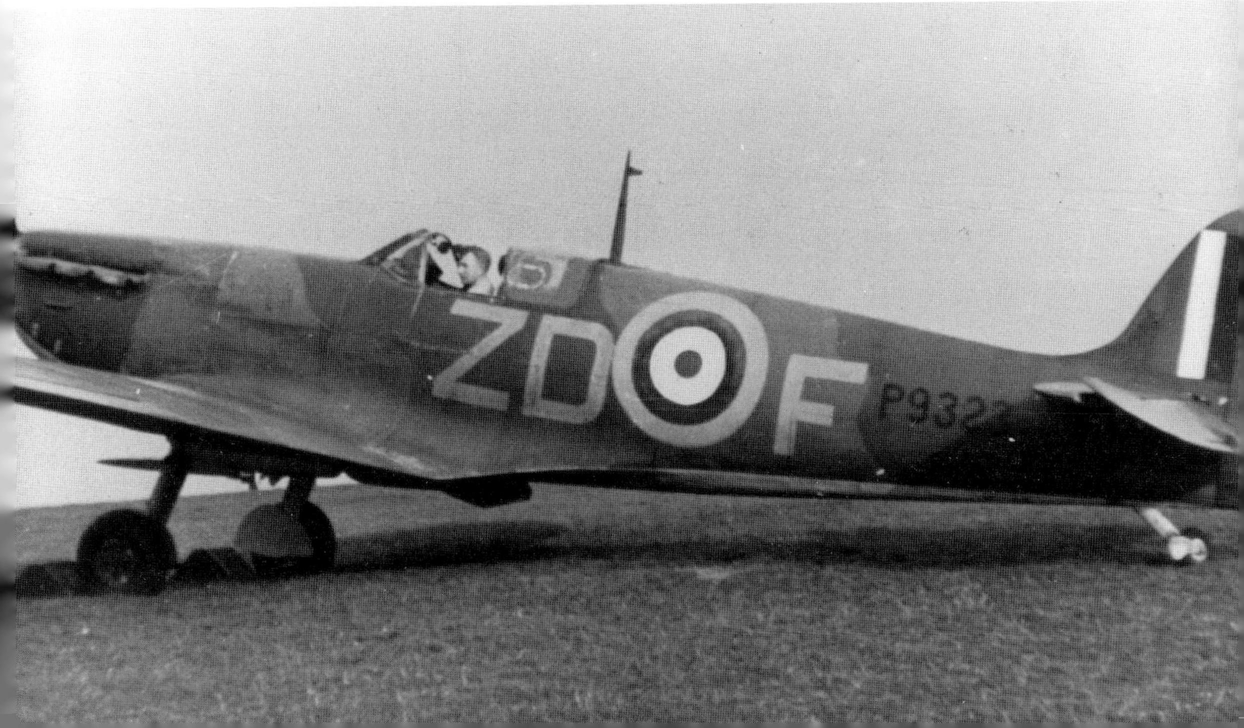

Ian L.M. Hallam was a doctor's son who joined the RAF on a Short Service Commission in 1937. Having served as an Army Cooperation pilot on Lysanders during the Fall of France, he volunteered to fly fighters and converted to Spitfires. By the end of September 1940, he was with 222 Squadron at Hornchurch and made a number of combat claims. In 1942, he was flying photographic reconnaissance Hurricanes over the western desert when brought down near Alamein and captured. Sadly, he was killed in a flying accident in 1952 when commanding the Aberdeen University Air Squadron at Dyce.

Flight Lieutenant Colin MacFie DFC, from Cheltenham, was a pre-war auxiliary pilot, originally with 611 Squadron, who saw action with 616 Squadron over Dunkirk, and later during the Battle of Britain. He would be shot down over France on 5 July 1941, and captured; he died in 1982.

The 611 Squadron Pilot's dispersal hut at Digby in Lincolnshire, circa 1940. Resting on the bed is Flying Officer Douglas 'Dirty' Watkins, a successful Spitfire pilot awarded the DFC; he survived the war but died in 1969. Second from right is Sergeant Alfred Burt, who flew Spitfires with 611 and 603 Squadrons in the Battle of Britain, with some success, before going overseas as a flying instructor. He remained in the post-war service and died in 1980.

Flying Officer Leonard Haines DFC of 19 Squadron, an early ace who was killed, along with his passenger, on 30 April 1941 when 'beating up' his new wife's home in a Miles Magister whilst instructing at Heston.

John Milne, who later became an architect, was a teenage airframe rigger on 19 Squadron during the Battle of Britain – and was devoted to the Spitfire and its august history.

John Joseph Jackson was an engine fitter on 610 'County of Chester' Squadron at Biggin Hill during the Battle of Britain; a married man, he was killed when the aerodrome was heavily bombed on 30 August 1940 and never met his second daughter, born a week later.

Ray Johnson was an armourer on 152 Squadron at Warmwell during the Battle of Britain, and later served in the Mediterranean and Far Eastern theatres.

The high morale of 152 Squadron's groundcrew at Warmwell is evident in this snapshot.

Pilot Officer Laurie Whitbread, from Ludlow in Shropshire, was a successful pilot on 222 Squadron over Dunkirk and during the Battle of Britain, until he was shot down in combat with Me 109s over Kent and killed on 20 September 1940.

Bob Beardsley was a pre-war volunteer reservist who found himself flying Spitfires with 610 Squadron at Biggin Hill and 41 Squadron at Hornchurch during the Battle of Britain. A successful fighter pilot, pictured here at Hornchurch during the Battle of Britain, he was awarded the DFC in 1941, and later served in North Africa and on the continent. Bob, who survived the war and became a teacher after leaving the RAF in 1970, died in 2003. A keen amateur photographer, this and a number of following photographs originated in his personal album.

41 Squadron's CO, Squadron Leader Don Finlay DFC, an Olympian, snapped by Bob Beardsley at Catterick.

Sergeant Herbert 'Mitch' Mitchell, a New Zealander serving on 41 Squadron, later reported missing over Malta with 603 Squadron on 12 May 1942.

Sergeant Terry Healey of 41 Squadron being 'photobombed' by Sergeant John Gilders at Hornchurch; he was killed over France flying Typhoon fighter-bombers in 1944.

Sergeant Len Thorne of 41 Squadron, pictured at Catterick in early 1941.

Sergeant John Gilders, who became an ace in the Battle of Britain with 41 Squadron, only to be reported missing on 21 February 1941, after his Spitfire dived into the ground, probably due to oxygen failure, at Chilham, Kent – the pilot would not be recovered, in fact, until 1994.

An unidentified 41 Squadron pilot from amongst Squadron Leader Bob Beardsley's photographs.

41 Squadron pilots at Hornchurch in late 1940; from left: Sergeant Robert Angus, and Pilot Officers Edward 'Hawkeye' Wells (an ace from New Zealand) and Roy Ford. Angus did not survive the war; he was reported missing over the Channel on 20 February 1941.

Sergeants Bob Beardsley, 'Mitch' Mitchell and Frank 'ITMA' Usmar of 41 Squadron at Catterick in early 1941. Usmar survived being shot down, wounded and mistaken for a German during the Battle of Britain; he remained in the post-war service and died peacefully in 1994.

Flight Lieutenant Pat Meagher of 41 Squadron at readiness, Hornchurch, 1940. A successful fighter pilot, he also destroyed a number of Japanese aircraft, ending the war a group captain decorated with the DSO and DFC.

A 41 Squadron sergeant-pilot at Catterick only identified on Bob Beardsley's album as 'Ray'.

Sergeant Norman 'Sticky' Glew pictured whilst serving with 41 Squadron at Catterick in early 1941; he was killed in a flying accident whilst commanding a squadron in Sicily on 17 May 1944.

An unidentified 41 Squadron pilot at readiness, Hornchurch, late 1940.

An unidentified 41 Squadron sergeant-pilot in the pilot's dispersal hut at Hornchurch.

Sergeants Tom Hindle and 'Sticky' Glew, Catterick, late 1940.

Two Canadian pilots serving with 41 Squadron at Hornchurch in 1941.

Sergeant Harry Fowler on readiness at Catterick.

After the formal handover to 41 Squadron at Catterick of Spitfire Mk IIA, P8044, EB-J, by Major General Pearks on behalf of the Canadian Army's 1st Division.

Sergeant 'Sticky' Glew snapped by Bob Beardsley from atop a Catterick blast pen.

48

Squadron Leader Don Finlay (standing, fourth from left), with 41 Squadron at Hornchurch in early 1941. From left, standing on Spitfire: Pilot Officers H.C. Baker, D.A. Adams, F.J. Aldridge; Sergeant E.V. Darling, Pilot Officer J.N. MacKenzie, Flight Lieutenant A.D.J. Lovell. Standing, from left: Pilot Officer D.E. Mileham, Flight Lieutenant E.N. Ryder, Sergeants R.A. Angus, T.W.R. Healey, J.S. Gilders; Pilot Officers E.P. Wells and R.C. Ford.

Line shoot: 41 Squadron chalking up victory claims on a panel from a Do 17 shot down over North Wales by Pilot Officer Denis Adams (pictured fourth from right, back row).

Flying Officer Bob Beardsley DFC pictured whilst instructing at a Spitfire conversion unit in 1942.

Two of Bob Beardsley's fellow Spitfire instructors: Flying Officer Alan Smith DFC at left, who had flown as Wing Commander Bader's No 2 in 'Dogsbody Section' of 616 Squadron at Tangmere in 1941.

Pilot Officer Hugh Reilley was a Canadian killed during the Battle of Britain on 17 October 1940, when shot down by Major Werner Mölders, Kommodore of JG 51. His story is told in the author's *Battle of Britain 1940: The Finest Hour's Human Cost* (2020), and at the time of writing moves are afoot to see a memorial erected near Reilley's crash-site in Kent.

Sergeant Leslie Allton flew Spitfires with 266 and 92 Squadrons but was killed when his Spitfire, R6692, crashed in Kent on 19 October 1940, apparently having been ambushed by an unseen German fighter. The 20-year-old was taken home and buried in Nuneaton, where Battle of Britain enthusiast Steve Jones ensures that his grave is well maintained today (London Battle of Britain Monument via Steve Jones).

Howard Frizelle 'Billy' Burton was a pre-war Cranwell Sword of Honour winner and undoubtedly destined for great things – but it was not to be. Having fought over Dunkirk as a flight commander with 66 Squadron, Billy was promoted to command 616 Squadron, which he went on to lead throughout the 'season' of 1941 as part of Wing Commander Bader's Tangmere Wing. Afterwards, he became a wing leader in North Africa, but was tragically amongst those officers reported missing when their unarmed Hudson was shot down over the Bay of Biscay whilst returning from home leave on 3 June 1943. His story is told in the author's *Forgotten Heroes of the Battle of Britain* (2022).

A senior NCO of 616 Squadron's ground staff at Tangmere 1941.

After tours at frontline fighter stations in the south-east, squadrons were rotated and rested away from the combat zone where they were able to receive and train new pilots. On 26 February 1941, 616 Squadron flew south from Kirton to Tangmere, exchanging its Spitfire Mk IAs for the IIAs of 65 Squadron, with which it swapped places. This is Sergeant A.H. Johnson (right) of 65 Squadron at Kirton, shortly after the exchange, with an unidentified Polish pilot. Johnson was later shot down over Le Touquet on 21 October 1941 and captured; he died in 1967.

Bob Morris was an 18-year-old RAF Halton engineering apprentice who served on 66 Squadron throughout the Battle of Britain. Arriving at Duxford to see lines of Spitfires, Bob was beside himself with excitement: 'Here', he told me, 'was every young man's dream'. Bob's love affair with the Spitfire endured a lifetime; he died in 2014.

After the Battle of Britain, 66 Squadron spent some time at RAF Exeter in 10 Group, where this photograph was taken in early 1941. The pilots include Battle of Britain veterans Sergeants Douggy Hunt (second left) and Jimmy 'Binder' Corbin (extreme right), both of whom featured in *Ten Fighter Boys*, published in 1942; both survived the war. The Spitfire is Mk IIA, P7843, LZ-C, 'Aldergrove', which was one of eighteen aircraft presented by the Belfast Telegraph's Spitfire Fund.

Jack Stokoe became an ace flying Spitfires with 603 Squadron during the Battle of Britain, during which he survived being shot down and wounded, as he did again in April 1941 when forced to bale out over the North Sea. Fortunately, Jack was rescued and survived the war as a squadron leader decorated with the DFC; he was later a trading standards officer and died in 1999.

Robert Harold 'Jack' Strang was a New Zealander from Invercargill who first flew Spitfires with 65 Squadron, before becoming a flight commander on Kenley's 485 (New Zealand) Squadron and was ultimately reported missing from a sweep over France on 25 January 1942. By that time, he had completed 67 operational sorties. Jack is pictured here when a pilot officer on 65 Squadron in an early Spitfire Mk I with the 'broom handle' radio mast and lacking a rear-view mirror.

Pilots of 65 'East India' Squadron at Hornchurch during the Battle of Britain, including the New Zealander Flying Officer Ron Wigg (extreme left) and Pilot Officer Robin Norwood (extreme right), both of whom survived the war.

After the Battle of Britain, 65 Squadron received and trained replacement pilots before returning to Tangmere, where two such young men, namely Sergeants Hugh Chalmers (left) and Peter Rose, are pictured early in 1941.

Well done Dilip!
Kind regards,
Hugh Chalmers
65 Sqdn. in 1940.

EAST INDIA SQUADRON

Sergeant Hugh Chalmers exiting his Spitfire at Tangmere, wearing privately purchased sheepskin gloves.

A Scot, Hugh Chalmers was later commissioned and also flew Spitfires over Malta. He survived the war to become a PE teacher and is pictured here when visiting the Battle of Britain Memorial Flight at Coningsby in the late 1980s.

Sergeant Rose was not as lucky as his friend Hugh Chalmers: Peter was lost whilst flying a photographic reconnaissance sortie over Belgium when engine failure forced him to take to his parachute, which failed to open. Another deeply moving story told in the author's *Spitfire Down* (2022).

EAST INDIA SQUADRON

Sergeant Ron Stillwell arrived on 65 Squadron as a replacement pilot during the Battle of Britain, and would see extensive action in the following years, being decorated with the DFM and DFC, and ultimately commanding 65 Squadron. He is pictured here with Spitfire Mk VB AA734, 'Calcutta', donated by the East India Fund for British War Services, in 1942. Ron survived the war; he died in 1993.

Pilots of 65 Squadron at Kirton, March 1941. Back row, from left: Pilot Officer Rathie, Sergeants Hewlett, Johnson and Mitchell, and Pilot Officer MacPherson; seated, from left: Flight Lieutenant Grant, Sergeants Rose, Oldnall, Stillwell and Foulgar.

Sergeant-pilots of 65 Squadron at readiness in 1941.

A 65 Squadron pilot and Spitfire Mk IIA, 1941.

The people of India's Sind province presented seven Spitfires under the auspices of Lord Beaverbrook's 'Spitfire Fund'; this is Sergeant Chris Oldnall of 65 Squadron with 'Sind V', Mk IIA P7836 at Tangmere early in 1941.

65 Squadron pilots at readiness in 1941, including, from left, Sergeant Vic Lowson, Pilot Officer Jack Strang, Flying Officer Tommy Smart, unknown (with pipe), and Flying Officer Brendan 'Paddy' Finucane DFC, the famous Irish ace.

A posed press photograph at Tangmere on 4 February 1941 – the pilots had been released and just off to Brighton when the photographers arrived, hence their smart uniforms! From left: Sergeants Harold Orchard and Hugh Chalmers, Flying Officers Paddy Finucane and Ron Wigg, and Sergeants Peter Rose and Peter Mitchell. Sergeant Orchard, one of The Few and a successful fighter pilot, was killed in action over France the following day in Spitfire P7733 and is buried at Neufchatel-Hardelot New Communal Cemetery; he was from Weymouth, Dorset, and 24 years old.

65 Squadron pilots at Kirton, spring 1941, including Sergeants Humphrey Baxter (second left), Ron Stillwell (fourth left) and Victor Lowson (second right). The tall officer is not a pilot but more likely the Squadron Adjutant or Intelligence Officer. The graffiti on their dispersal hut is definitely unofficial!

Sergeant Stillwell prepares to take-off in YT-X.

65 Squadron's commander, Squadron Leader Gerald Saunders (third from right), at Tangmere in January 1941 with, from left, Pilot Officer Victor Lowson, Sergeant Ron Stillwell, Flying Officer Tommy Smart, Pilot Officer Robin Norwood and Flying Officer Paddy Finucane DFC. The significance of the 'For Sale' sign is unknown!

Another snapshot of Squadron Leader Saunders and pilots, at Kirton (sixth from left). Pilot Officer MacPherson is second left, Pilot Officer Norwood fourth left; kneeling, from left, are Sergeants Baxter, Chalmers and Lowson, Stillwell (and an unknown pilot).

Victor Lowson, a volunteer reservist from Dundee, was later commissioned but reported missing after a low-level attack on Zeebrugge on 21 July 1942. Hit by machine-gun fire upon crossing the enemy coast, 'Vicky' turned out to sea but as he prepared to bale out, his Spitfire dived into the North Sea. The popular pilot, whose loss was keenly felt on 65 Squadron, was never seen again and is remembered on the Runnymede Memorial to missing British and Commonwealth aircrew.

Pilot Officer Robin Norwood of 65 Squadron at Tangmere in January 1941.

In April 1941, Paddy Finucane was promoted to flight lieutenant and became a flight commander on the newly formed 452 (Australian) Squadron. On 21 July 1941, 452 Squadron moved to Kenley, where this photograph was taken of Finucane congratulating a sergeant-pilot after a successful combat. On 21 June 1942, Finucane, decorated with the DSO and DFC, and amongst the leading aces, was promoted to command the Kenley Wing – but was lost on 15 July 1942, on a 'Rhubarb' low-level nuisance raid. Hit by machine-gun fire over Le Touquet, with his collant system damaged, Paddy headed back out to sea and ditched his Spitfire – which sank like a stone before he had chance to escape the cockpit. The gallant Irishman was never found and is also remembered on Runnymede.

As Fighter Command took the war across the Channel in 1941, so many highly experienced fighter pilots and leaders were lost on these arguably senseless operations – amongst them the highly decorated ace Flight Lieutenant Eric 'Sawn-Off' Lock, who was also hit by ground fire over the French coast, on 3 August 1941, and never seen again; it is assumed that his Spitfire crashed into the Channel. He is pictured here at Hornchurch earlier that fateful year.

Peter Devitt was a pre-war reserve officer and auxiliary who was posted to command 152 Squadron in March 1940. The Squadron saw much action over the West Country, flying from Warmwell, inland of Weymouth, during the Battle of Britain. Devitt later served in the Far East and re-joined the Auxiliary Air Force post-war, commanding 615 Squadron; he died in 1997.

Amongst Squadron Leader Devitt's pilots on 152 Squadron was the mercurial Pilot Officer Eric 'Boy' Marrs DFC (second right, front row). After a number of combat successes, Marrs was shot down by flak whilst escorting bombers on a raid to Brest on 24 June 1941; he is buried at Kerfautras Cemetery.

The Supermarine factory at Woolston proved too small an operation to produce the numbers of Spitfires required in wartime, and being just sixty miles due south of Cherbourg it was vulnerable to enemy air attack. Consequently, Lord Nuffield was tasked with turning the Morris Motor Works at Castle Bromwich, Birmingham, over to producing Spitfires en masse. After initial teeting problems the massive factory was soon in full-swing – and ultimately produced the majority of 22,000 Spitfires built. These aircraft were all subjected to rigorous flight testing before handing over to the RAF, this unsung and often daneregous work being led by record-breaking pre-war civilian pilot Alex Henshaw, pictured here (right) with Czech test pilot Flight Lieutenant Venda Jicha DFC. Jicha, an ace and one of The Few, was resting between operational tours whilst serving as a test pilot under Henshaw. Sadly, Jicha was killed in a flying accident whilst travelling from Castle Bromwich to Kinloss on 1 February 1945.

The British Prime Minister, Winston Churchill, visiting Castle Bromwich and in conversation with the Chief Test Pilot, Alex Henshaw.

Whether the labrador actually flew with Alex Henshaw in this Spitfire is a matter of conjecture!

Spitfire production, from the centres at Southampton and Castle Bromwich, was sensibly dispersed, with sub-assemblies and parts being constructed at diverse locations, including garages and even under railway arches. It is also noteworthy that many workers producing Spitfires were women, the men being away in the services. These ladies are producing Spitfire wing leading edges and hydraulic piping at the former Rackstraw's cabinet-making works in Loves Grove, Worcester. Weekly, the completed sub-assemblies were collected and conveyed to the Castle Bromwich Aircraft Factory.

Without doubt, the 'Spitfire Fund' was a stroke of genius. Lord Beaverbrook, the Minister for Aircraft Production, implored housewives to donate pots and pans, from which, he said, Spitfires would be made. This was not actually true, because the aluminium used in the production of cooking utensils is not of the high grade required for aircraft production – but, nonetheless, the initiative provided the Home Front with a means of hitting back at German bombers. Soon, veritable mountains of pots and pans developed.

The Spitfire Fund also captured the imagination of free people all over the world, who competed to collect the £5,000 'The Beaver' placed on a Spitfire, so that an aircraft could be 'presented' and bear the donor's name. Amongst the first were those donated by the Worcester Evening News and Times Spitfire Fund, this being Mk IIA, P8046, 'City of Worcester II', which was built at Castle Bromwich.

On 26 August 1941, P8046 was being flown by Sergeant Cliff Jacka of 234 Squadron during a low-level attack on the enemy airfield at Maupertus, near Cherbourg. Jacka's Spitfire was hit by flak and crashed near the airfield, killing the pilot, a 24-year-old volunteer reservist and motorcycle enthusiast from Bournemouth.

Sergeant Peter Fox, one of The Few (kneeling at front left whilst serving with 234 Squadron at Warmwell in 1941), was flying with Sergeant Jacka when he was killed, and the 20-year-old had the unenviable duty of personally informing his friend's parents, who ran a bed and breakfast in the popular Dorset seaside town of Bournemouth. On 20 October 1941, Peter was shot down himself over France but managed to crash-land and was captured; a surveyor post-war, he died in 2005.

Another of those early presentation Spitfires was Mk IIA P8047, 'The Malverns', presented by the Malvern Gazette newspaper. The aircraft had a long service history, seeing action with 74 Squadron, and was eventually scrapped in 1944 following a flying accident.

Sergeant Cedric Stone of 72 Squadron at Biggin Hill in 1941. Having seen action over France during the Non-Stop Offensive of 1941, he was posted to North Africa in April 1943, to fly Hurricanes with 73 Squadron, describing this, after Spitfires, as 'a terrible come down'.

An excellent snapshot, taken by Pilot Officer Wallace 'Jock' Cunningham DFC of his 19 Squadron friend Pilot Officer Michael Tucker, who was sadly killed in action on 21 July 1941 and buried at Becklingen War Cemetery, Germany.

Sergeant David Denchfield of Tangmere's 610 Squadron was amongst the so-called 'Non-Stop Offensive's' early casualties when shot down over France and captured on 2 February 1941. He survived the war and died in 2012.

Sergeant Bob Morton, 616 Squadron, Tangmere 1941: 'My mother asked me to have a portrait photograph taken – so I did!'

Sergeant Alan Smith of 616 Squadron at Tangmere in 1941, when he frequently flew as wingman to Wing Commander Douglas Bader. Later commissioned and decorated with the DFC, Alan did well over Malta. After the war he enjoyed a long career in business, for which he received a knighthood; he died in 2013.

Sergeant Frank Twitchett was a replacement pilot towards the end of the Battle of Britain and, in 1941, flew Spitfires with 145 Squadron in the Tangmere Wing.

On 21 June 1941, 145 Squadron was in combat with Me 109s over France, and Sergeant Twitchett was shot-up by Oberleutnant Matzke of II/JG 26. Although wounded he managed to return Spitfire Mk IIA P8341, SO-J, to Merston – where flight rigger Dave Horne pokes his head through the damaged tail. Any suggestion that the Spitfire was unable to absorb combat damage and keep flying is unsupported by the actual evidence available – as is so often the case.

Pilots of 234 Squadron in 1941.

A member of 616 Squadron's groundcrew in 1942 points to a four-leafed clover painted on a Spitfire's tail – but would the talisman be sufficient to bring the pilot enough luck to survive unscathed?

Armourers at work.

An armourer at Biggin Hill demonstrates just how big the 20mm Hispano-Suiza cannon was – 7 feet long and weighing 96lb each.

Armorers at Biggin Hill replenishing a Spitfire's cannon ammunition drum with 20mm rounds.

Armourers during the course of re-fitting a Hispano 20mm ammunition drum.

A Spitfire Mk VB of the Czech 310 Squadron being re-fuelled. It is easy to forget that the essential groundcrews often worked long hours out in the open, in all weathers.

A camera being fitted to a Photographic Reconnaissance Unit Spitfire – the motto of which was 'Unarmed and unafraid'. Brave men indeed, flying deep into enemy territory to gather essential intelligence.

So many pilots were killed during training, in flying accidents, without ever firing a shot at the enemy. This is 22-year-old Sergeant Donald John MacKenzie, who was killed whilst converting to Spitfires at 61 Operational Training Unit, Rednal, on 10 July 1942. The aircraft concerned, X4644, which had seen action with 611 Squadron, was rather tired, having been taken on charge in October 1940, and on the fateful day the pilot suffered an engine fire. Unfortunately, Sergeant MacKenzie crashed and was killed whilst attempting a forced-landing at Gadlas Farm, near Ellesmere, Shropshire. X4644 was a presentation aircraft, 'Sarkar-I-Tirhut' (meaning 'Thunderbird') and one of two donated by the Maharaja of Dharbanga in Bihar, India. They took young Donald back home to Stornoway and buried him in the Scottish island's Sandwick cemetery.

In 1942, Lesley Howard's film *First of The Few*, a somewhat romanticised version of the R.J. Mitchell and creation of the Spitfire stories, was premiered and became one of the Second World War's biggest grossing films. Starring Howard as Mitchell, and David Niven as Supermarine test pilot 'Geoffrey Crisp', 118 Squadron supplied the Spitfires for flying scenes, which were filmed at RAF Ibsley in Hampshire. Amongst the pilots involved was Flight Lieutenant Peter Howard-Williams DFC, one of The Few, who was a keen photographer and whose snapshots we see here. This was taken of Howard, who also produced and directed the film, by another pilot using Peter's camera; Peter can be seen at right in the background with his friend Flying Officer John Robson DFC, who also flew for the cameras.

Flight Lieutenant Peter Howard-Williams in conversation with Lesley Howard at Ibsley.

Lesley Howard in conversation with Flying Officer Robson (left) and Flight Lieutenant Peter Howard-Williams.

Flight Sergeant Lewis, the NCO of 118 Squadron's 'A' Flight groundcrew, and Pilot Officer Walter Milne with Lesley Howard at Ibsley.

Flight Sergeant Lewis and Pilot Officer Walter Milne, both of 118 Squadron, with a 501 Squadron Spitfire; 501 were sharing Ibsley with 118 at the time.

Lesley Howard enjoying some banter with pilots of 118 and possibly 501 Squadron.

Tea-break between takes.

The film's opening scenes include actual Ibsley Spitfire pilots discussing the R.J. Mitchell and Spitfire story, including a number of The Few. Here, Lesley Howard directs Flying Officer David Fulford DFC (left), who had flown with 19 Squadron during the Battle of Britain, and a most distinguished veteran of the air battles in 1940, namely Squadron Leader Christopher 'Bunny' Currant DFC, who was commanding 501 Squadron at Ibsley when the film was made.

Lesley Howard directing the scene wherein a shot-up squadron commander crash-lands his Spitfire. David Niven is in civilian dress with sunglasses, standing with the pilot concerned, another distinguished member of The Few, Wing Commander Frank Howell DFC – who would survive years of deprivation as a prisoner of the Japanese, only to die in a tragic flying related accident in 1948. The aircraft is another presentation Spitfire, Mk VB P8789, 'Borough of Wanstead and Woodford', which was on charge with 118 Squadron but had suffered an undercarriage collapse on 26 September 1941. After use in the film and repair, the Spitfire resumed operational flying, but was lost on 1 June 1942 when its engine failed, causing Flight Sergeant Ron Stillwell of 65 Squadron (who appears elsewhere in this book) to bale out into the sea – fortunately the pilot was rescued two hours later.

An unidentified pilot of 118 Squadron from Wing Commander Howard-Williams' album, with Spitfire P8376 'Sinaboong', donated by the Netherlands East Indies, which ultimately perished in a mid-air collision over Hampshire on 30 June 1941.

Four 118 Squadron sergeant-pilots with P8376 NK–Z 'Sinaboong' at Ibsley.

'Sinaboong' became the personal Spitfire of Flying Officer Peter Howard-Williams for a time, seen here sitting on the aircraft's wing. He has added the unofficial name 'Sheila', this being a girlfriend at the time.

Another Peter Howard-Williams 118 Squadron Ibsley snapshot; from left: Pilot Officers Vanstae (Dutch) and Jones, and Sergeant HC Kerr (Canadian, missing 29 January 1942); on wing: Pilot Officer Ted Ames (Canadian, missing, 2 February 1942) and Pilot Officer Don Claxton (missing, 25 April 1942).

The 'Baby of the RAF': Sergeant Geoffrey Painting, the youngest pilot ever to be killed flying with the RAF, who was shot down by flak during an attack on flak ships off Cherbourg on 30 September 1941. Sergeant Painting was flying as No 2 to Flight Lieutenant Peter Howard-Williams DFC at the time. He remains missing; his moving story is told in this author's *Spitfire Down* (2022).

Flight Lieutenant Johnnie Johnson DFC (in cockpit) with pilots and groundcrew of his 'B' Flight of 616 Squadron at King's Cliffe, May 1942. The aircraft is Mk VB AA879, YQ-U, which was later struck off charge owing to combat damage beyond economical repair whilst on charge with 118 Squadron.

Flight Lieutenant Johnnie Johnson DFC at King's Cliffe in May 1942 with his rigger, Arthur Radcliffe (left) and fitter, Fred Burton. A gifted leader, Johnnie, who survived the war as the RAF's officially top-scoring fighter pilot and eventually retired as an air vice-marshal, remained lifelong friends with these men. This period of his wartime flying days is covered in *Johnnie Johnson's 1942 Diary* (2021), introduced and edited by this author.

Another ace: Squadron Leader Don Kingaby DSO DFM*, commander of 122 Squadron at Hornchurch in 1943. Known as the '109 Specialist', his final score was twenty-one German aircraft destroyed with two more shared, six probables and eleven damaged. His Spitfire is emblazoned with his personal motif, a tally of his aerial victories to date and squadron leader's pennant. Don survived the war and died in the USA in 1990.

Pilot Officer Ken Wilkinson (standing on wing and leaning on windscreen) was another of The Few, having been posted as a replacement pilot to 19 Squadron at Fowlmere towards the end of the Battle of Britain. This photograph, of 165 Squadron's 'A' Flight with a Spitfire Mk IX was taken at Church Stanton in 1943. Ken survived the war and became a great ambassador for the Battle of Britain Fighter Association; he died in 2017.

Many pilots trained overseas under the auspices of the Empire Air Training Scheme. Welshman George Lock (left) won his wings at the American Army Air Corps Advanced Flying School at Napier Field, Dothan, Alabama, and is pictured here, with Sergeant Kelly, after being presented with both RAF and USAAC 'wings' by the Director of Training, Lieutenant-Colonel Williams, on 6 February 1942. The proud new pilots are wearing both sets of wings.

Sergeant George Lock pictured upon his return to England with his sister, Joan, in London. George was posted to the Telecommunications Unit at RAF Defford, Worcestershire, which provided aircraft for the Malvern-based Telecommunications Research Establishment's experiments and trials. Defford accommodated a vast array of many kinds of aircraft, and George regularly flew Bristol Beaufighters on Airborne Interception radar trials, and Spitfires, of the Station Defence Flight, which were also used as 'targets' in such experiments.

Not far from RAF Defford was RAF Perdiswell, on the outskirts of Worcester, home to 2 Elementary Flying Training Unit. On 26 February 1943, a young Australian, Sergeant J.F.C. MacPherson, was up from Perdiswell, practising aerobatics in a Tiger Moth. Sergeant George Lock took off from Defford in Spitfire X4918, made his left turn to leave the circuit – and collided with the biplane. MacPherson baled out safely, but the 21-year-old George Lock was killed. On 31 May 1943, however, whilst Sergeant MacPherson was converting to Spitfires at Rednal, near Oswestry, his Spitfire, X4930, collided with a Mosquito over Shrewsbury, resulting in the deaths of all aircrew involved. MacPherson was buried at Oswestry Cemetery, another young man far from home. The white flash in his forage cap indicates a pilot under training.

Wing Leader Peter Malam Brothers was an experienced pre-war pilot who distinguished himself during the Fall of France and Battle of Britain. By October 1942 he was leading the Tangmere Wing, where he is pictured here, his Spitfire bearing victory symbols and his wing commander's pennant. Peter survived the war with a DSO and DFC and Bar, with a final tally of sixteen enemy aircraft destroyed, one probable and three damaged. He remained in the post-war service, eventually retiring as an air commodore, and in more recent years was an enthusiastic Chairman of the Battle of Britain Fighter Association; he died in 2008.

Thomas Henry Desmond Drinkwater was a butcher who joined the RAF as an aircraft-hand in 1936, training as a rigger. In 1940, he made the quantum leap to become a fighter pilot, and after training, joined 234 Squadron at Warmwell in June 1941. 'Drink', pictured here as a newly arrived sergeant-pilot at Warmwell, would find himself hotly engaged with the enemy for most of the war.

On 23 June 1942, the Portreath and Exeter Spitfire Wings clashed with FW190s of III/JG 2 off Start Point after which Oberleutnant Arnim Faber became disorientated, mistaking the Bristol for the English Channel and landing at RAF Pembrey in South Wales – thus presenting the RAF with an intact 'Butcher Bird' for evaluation. This was truly significant, as the FW190 was causing major problems at the time, and this was the first example the Allies had been able to examine. Flight Lieutenant Drinkwater was flying that day and is pictured here with Faber's 190 at Pembrey. A Beaufighter night-fighter can be seen in the background.

Another of 'Drink's' snapshots from that day at Pembrey, this officer standing by a Spitfire simply recorded as 'A Station Officer, Pembrey'.

The same officer, a pilot decorated with the DFC, in conversation with 'two Canadian pilots' at Pembrey.

The 'Station Officer', who appears to be holding a cane, with the Canadian pilot appearing at left in the previous photograph – note the 'Canada' arm flash.

The same pilot, of 234 Squadron (code AZ), whose Spitfire is unofficially named 'Daphne'.

Flight Lieutenant Drinkwater DFC pictured whilst commanding 19 Squadron's 'B' Flight in 1943.

On 11 November 1943, Flight Lieutenant Drinkwater destroyed 19 Squadron's 10th enemy aircraft, a FW190. He is seen here (left) cutting the celebratory cake held by the Squadron Commander, Squadron Leader Vic Ekins DFC, who had flown Hurricanes during the Battle of Britain with 501 Squadron. In January 1944, 19 Squadron's long association with the Spitfire ended when the type was replaced by the P-51 Mustang III. In April 1944, 'Drink' was promoted to squadron leader and took command of 122 Squadron, also flying Mustangs. Sadly, on 14 May 1944, Squadron Leader Drinkwater was shot down by flak during a low-level 'Ranger' operation near Nantes, and killed; a married man, his brother read 'Drink's' last letter home to his wife, 'Wilf', in the final episode of the acclaimed *World at War* television documentary series. This author told the story most recently in *Spitfire Voices* (2010).

Pilot Officer Réne Rogér, a Free French pilot serving with 19 Squadron, pictured with Spitfire Mk VB, EP445.

In that universal sign language of fighter pilots, Pilot Officer Réne Rogér shows how to get on an enemy aircraft's tail. Sadly, he was killed right at the war's end in an accident whilst flying home to see his parents in France.

More universal sign language from an unidentified 72 Squadron flight lieutenant at Biggin Hill in 1941.

Group Captain 'Sailor' Malan, a South African, remains a legendary name amongst fighter pilots, particularly from the early war period when he commanded 74 Squadron and the Biggin Hill Wing. He later commanded that station and is seen here during that time, in 1943, with the Jamaican Flight Sergeant Vincent Bunting of 611 Squadron. Before the war, Malan had travelled widely as a mercantile marine officer, and developed an early worldview. Opposed to any kind of injustice, after the war he returned to South Africa and actively campaigned against apartheid – the full story is told in this author's *Sailor Malan: Freedom Fighter* (2021).

A photograph emphasising the diverse nations which combined to fly and fight against Germany with the RAF: Group Captain Malan (left) with Squadron Leader Jack Charles DFC, a Canadian commanding 611 Squadron, and the Biggin Hill Wing Leader, the New Zealand ace Wing Commander Alan Deere DFC, Biggin Hill, 1943.

An historic photograph: Group Captain Malan, Station Commander at Biggin Hill (fifth from right), on the occasion of the Station's 1,000th aerial victory, 15 May 1943, with the two pilots who jointly shared that honour, the Free Frenchman Commandant Réne Mouchotte (to Malan's right) and Squadron Leader Jack Charles (to Mouchotte's right).

Pilots of the Air Transport Auxiliary – 164 of which were female – did incredible work delivering aircraft to the squadrons, wherever in the world they may be and in all weathers. This is Maureen Dunlop, born in Argentina to an Australian father and English mother. She learned to fly in Argentina in 1936, travelling to England and joining the ATA in 1942. Largely flying with the all-female Ferry Pool at Hamble, Maureen flew thirty-eight different types of aircraft, including many Spitfires, logging 800 flying hours. In 1944, she became a pin-up girl when appearing on the front cover of *Picture Post*; she died, aged 91, in 2012.

Second Officer Helen Marcelle Harrison, pictured here with a Spitfire Mk IX, was a pioneering female Canadian pilot and the first Canadian female to serve in the ATA; she died in 1995 after a lifetime in aviation, and was inducted into Canada's Aviation Hall of Fame in 1974.

Martyn Steynor, from Malvern, Worcestershire, was a pre-war civilian pilot too old for frontline operational flying when the Second World War broke out. Instead, Martyn immediately joined the ATA, and is seen here loading his kit into an Anson, ready to be flown with other pilots to ferry aircraft to the RAF. During the war, Martyn flew every conceivable type of Allied aircraft and was well-known locally for 'buzzing' the clock tower in North Malvern Road in a Sterling bomber!

Martyn Steynor was another devoted Spitfire enthusiast. He is pictured here, on the right, with former German He 111 pilot and prisoner of war Paul Moeller at one of this author's events in 1998; both airmen are now deceased.

Squadron Leader Colin Grey DFC, a New Zealander (in greatcoat) pictured at King's Cliffe whilst commanding 616 Squadron in 1942. The pilots are from Flight Lieutenant Johnnie Johnson DFC's 'B' Flight (third left) and include the Canadian, Pilot Officer Bob 'Trapper' Bowen (second left). The other pilots, from left, are described in Johnnie's album as 'Tess, Bolton, Winter and Strouts'.

Pilot Officer Bob 'Trapper' Bowen, a Canadian pictured whilst serving with 616 Squadron in 1942.

During the Battle of Britain, Piotr Laguna flew Hurricanes with 302 (Polish) Squadron at Duxford, and the following year became leader of No 1 Polish Fighter Wing based at Northolt. On 27 June 1941, Wing Commander Laguna's Spitfire, P8331, 'Sumatra', was hit by ground-fire during a low-level attack on a German airfield near Calais, the highly respected pilot being killed in the resulting crash. Many years later the wreckage of his aircraft was acquired by Scott Booth and now forms the basis of the Laguna's Spitfire Legacy Project – which will one day hopefully see this Spitfire Mk IIB airworthy once more. The story is told in this author's *Spitfire Down* (2022).

Another early Polish arrival in England was Jurek Poplawski, who first flew Hurricanes during the Battle of Britain before joining 308 Squadron at Baginton in spring 1941, and subsequently becoming an ace at Northolt later that year (where this photograph was taken). Squadron Leader Poplawski survived the war and emigrated to Buenos Aires, where he died in 2004. His story is told in this author's *Letters From The Few* (2020).

By the spring of 1941, an increasing number of squadrons comprising foreign nationals were working up on Spitfires, amongst them the Polish 308 'City of Krakow' Squadron, pilots of which are pictured here at the famous Baginton Oak landmark, adjacent to their nearby airfield, in late 1940, whilst still flying Hurricanes. The Squadron would soon move to Northolt, joining No 1 Polish Fighter Wing, and these men would see relentless action over France during the months and years ahead. Amongst those pictured are Pilot Officers Felix Szyszka (in forage cap, behind Flight Lieutenant Jasionowski, holding dog) and Stanislaw Wandzilak (extreme right, front row). Among the men in this image is, at extreme left back, Flying Officer Stanislaw Weilgus. Likewise, between and just behind the two officers in the foreground wearing peaked caps, leaning forward wearing a forage cap and Irvin jacket, is Sergeant Tadeuz Heganbarth. Both Weilgus and Heganbarth would soon be killed in action.

Amongst 308 Squadron's original pilots was Flying Officer Stanislaw Weilgus, who would lose his life in combat with Me 109s over France on 12 July 1941.

Pilot Officer Bruno Kudrewicz shared a room with Flying Officer Weilgus at Northolt, so 'felt his loss most keenly'. Bruno survived flying Spitfires and Mustangs throughout the war, after which he became a publican in Thatcham before emigrating to New Zealand.

Pilot Officer Wladyslaw Bozek, also of 308 Squadron, who would be killed in action over France on 22 July 1941.

Pilot Officer Stanislaw Wandzilak of 308 Squadron preparing for a sweep from Northolt in 1941 – the chequered square is the red and white badge of the Polish Air Force and usually seen painted on the aircraft's nose, below the exhausts, so this position is very unusual. Wandzilak survived the war and retired as a group captain decorated with the DFC and post-war honours.

Pilot Officer Aleksander Wroblewski of Northolt-based 303 Squadron, who was shot-up in Spitfire Mk IIB P8208 on 13 June 1941, safely making a forced landing near Dover.

A Polish fighter legend: Group Captain Alexander Gabziewicz, a highly decorated Spitfire ace thought to be totally fearless; after the war he settled in Malvern, Worcestershire, where he died in 1983.

Pilot Officer R.S. Paderewski of 303 Squadron at Northolt during the relentless air-fighting of 1941.

Sergeants Giermer and Popek, both of 303 Squadron, at Northolt in 1941.

New Year's Eve celebration for 308 Squadron and guests at Leamington Spa's Clarendon Hotel – for some, this would be their last New Year.

Kazek Budzik joined 308 Squadron at Northolt in 1941, flying throughout the war with various Polish squadrons. He is pictured here in the Netherlands on 29 October 1944, literally a few minutes before being shot down by ground fire whilst strafing German positions. He safely force-landed near the Breda-Dordrecht bridge and was back in action two days later.

Kazek Budzik survived the war as a flight lieutenant, commanding a flight in 303 Squadron, and saw much action throughout the war. He is seen here being decorated with the Polish Virtuti Militari.

Flight Lieutenant Budzik married Helen, a Polish WAAF based at 12 Group HQ, Hucknall. After the war, the couple settled and raised a family in Nottingham. Kazek's father and brother, both army officers, were murdered by the Soviets at Katyn, and his mother's advice was not to come home but to remain in England. Kazek became a bus and coach driver, but never forgot his time flying Spitfires and Mustangs; he died in 2014. This author most recently told his story in *Spitfire Voices* (2010).

David Cox (left) was the first RAFVR sergeant-pilot posted to 19 Squadron, with which he served throughout the Battle of Britain. After participating in the offensive operations over France in 1941, the following year, by which time he had been commissioned, David went to North Africa, commanding a flight in Squadron Leader Bob Oxspring DFC's 72 Squadron. 'Oxo' had flown Spitfires during the Battle of Britain with 66 Squadron, and is pictured here congratulating Flight Lieutenant Cox on the award of his DFC in the western desert 1943.

The famous Stanley Devon photograph of Squadron Leader Brian Lane DFC taken at Fowlmere on 21 September 1940 is well-known – this is a unique snapshot from Brian's widow's estate of him in the western desert, circa 1942. Ill-health led to his return home, and tragically he was shot down over the North Sea and reported missing on 13 December 1942. The story is told, in detail, in this author's *Spitfire! The Unique Story of a Unique Battle of Britain Fighter Squadron* (2019).

Desert ace: Wing Commander Ian Gleed DSO DFC, another Battle of Britain ace. He was shot down and killed over Tunisia on 16 April 1943, leaving behind an excellent first-hand account, *Arise to Conquer*, recently re-released with an introduction and extra detail by this author and with eighty extra photographs.

Leading Aircraftman Maurice Leo, pictured by a Hurricane at Takali, in Malta, where he worked on Spitfires too, including those of 249 Squadron, throughout the great siege.

A Spitfire undergoing maintenance work at Takali, from Jon Leo's album.

Another Leo snapshot, two groundcrew colleagues and Spitfire Mk VC at Takali.

A Spitfire being rapidly re-armed and re-fuelled at the height of Malta's battering.

Malta ace: the Rhodesian Wing Commander John Agorastos Plagis, who was of Hellenic origin. His final score was over fifteen enemy aircraft destroyed, probably destroyed or damaged, and he survived the war.

Flight Lieutenant Lester Sanders DFC was an experienced pilot who also saw action over Malta, and survived being shot down on 8 July 1942, safely ditching Spitfire BR108 off Gozo. The aircraft was recovered by divers in 1973, and is now displayed at Malta's National War Museum. Sadly, Sanders did not survive the war: he was killed in a flying accident whilst serving as a test pilot under Alex Henshaw at Castle Bromwich on 23 October 1942. Another moving story included in this author's *Spitfire Down* (2022).

The defence of Malta was successfully coordinated by Air Vice-Marshal Sir Keith Park, one of the primary architects of victory in the Battle of Britain. Unlike most other officers in senior command positions, Park could actually fly the new monoplane fighters, and saw the Battle of Britain close-up in his personal Hurricane, whilst on Malta he famously flew a Spitfire.

A Mancunian, Ron 'Cloudy' Rayner was a volunteer reservist who first joined 41 Squadron at Catterick in early 1941. He went with the Squadron to Tangmere later that year, surviving being shot-up over France to crash-land at Hawkinge, before being commissioned and serving in North Africa, Sicily and Italy with 43 and 72 Squadrons. During this time Ron saw the air war over the north-west unfold and change in nature, the focus becoming close air support.

Whilst engaged on a ground-attack sortie when based at Ravenna in 1945, Flight Lieutenant Rayner's Spitfire Mk IX was damaged by flak – his groundcrew posing here with the machine, which Ron managed to get back safely. Ron survived the war with a DFC to his credit and afterwards became a jeweller before retiring to Malvern in Worcestershire. The author most recently told his story in *Spitfire Voices* (2010).

From Flight Lieutenant Ron Rayner DFC's album: Flying Officer Harry Lee, a volunteer reserve pilot flying Spitfires with 43 Squadron in Tunisia, 1942.

Another photograph from the Rayner album: Flight Lieutenant Robert 'Paddy' Turkington, an Irishman from Lurgan, whilst serving with 72 Squadron in Italy during 1944. Credited with the destruction of eight enemy aircraft, Turkington was awarded a DFC and Bar, and appointed to the DSO. Sadly, he was killed in a flying accident shortly before the war in Europe concluded. His medals were auctioned by the family in 2017 for £22,000.

Amongst the original Spitfire pilots on 19 Squadron back in 1938 was one Eric 'Tommy' Thomas, who later flew as a flight commander on 222 Squadron during the Battle of Britain and became an ace, decorated with the DFC and DSO, amongst other awards. This photograph was taken whilst he was commanding the Biggin Hill Wing in 1943, alongside his personal Spitfire Mk IX, bearing his initials: 'EHT', which was the wing leader's privilege. The following year he was invalided out of the service suffering with TB, and died prematurely in 1959. His story is appropriately included in this author's *Forgotten Heroes of the Battle of Britain* (2022).

Opposite and above: Squadron Leader Bernard Duperier, commanding 340 (Free French) Squadron in Wing Commander Eric Thomas's Biggin Hill Wing.

Also from Wing Commander Thomas's album, two Polish pilots of 306 'Torun' Squadron with what appears to be some kind of mascot alluding to the Squadron's crest.

Pilot Officer Frantisek Mlejnecky was a Free Czech who flew Spitfires with 310 and 312 (Czech) Squadrons: 'From my logbook: 312 Squadron, 26 August 1943, scramble 20,000 feet, Skaebrae. The Spitfire is a high-altitude Mk VII with a pressurised cockpit, the groundcrew having to bolt down the canopy, which can be seen on the ground. We were there to intercept high-flying German reconnaissance aircraft, although I saw nothing on this occasion'.

Flying Officer Robert Martin Davidson of 222 Squadron at Hornchurch in 1943, with Spitfire Mk IX MA509, 'Uruguay XVI'. Davidson was killed on 6 April 1945, flying a Hawker Tempest Mk V.

Allied fighter bombers ruled the skies over Normandy after D-Day, Allied aircraft being so numerous that to assist identification black and white 'D-Day stripes' were applied to wings and fuselages. This is Wing Commander Geoffrey Page DSO DFC setting off for an 'armed reconnaissance' over Normandy, his Spitfire carrying two 250lb bombs and a 500lb one. Page was shot down and horrendously burned flying Hurricanes in the Battle of Britain, requiring reconstruction of body and soul by Archibald McIndoe's famous Burns Unit at the Royal Victoria Hospital, East Grinstead. There, Page became a founder member of the Guinea Pig Club, for aircrew suffering disfiguring injuries who were treated by McIndoe. He survived the war and in later life was instrumental in seeing the National Memorial to The Few built at Capel-le-Ferne, now managed and maintained by the Battle of Britain Memorial Trust. He died in 2000.

By 1943, Johnnie Johnson was leading the Canadian Wing at Kenley. A highly popular and natural leader, Johnnie, who was not from a privileged background himself, cared not where a man was from or what he had materially, only whether he was 'reliable', and was loved for it.

The snapshot that says it all: Wing Commander Johnnie Johnson (centre, wearing Canada shoulder flashes presented by his pilots) at Kenley, anxiously awaiting an overdue pilot with Flight Lieutenants Norman Fowlow (left) and Dagwood Phillips.

Wing Commander Johnson (extreme right) at Kenley with Flight Lieutenants Dean MacDonald, Bob Bowen, Hugh Godefroy and Walter Conrad.

Johnnie Johnson's great friend, Squadron Leader Danforth Browne DFC, an American serving in the RCAF and commanding 441 Squadron at Kenley, with his groundcrew.

Squadron Leader Syd Ford and Flight Lieutenant Charlie Magwood at Kenley, 1943.

Flight Lieutenant Dean MacDonald DFC of 403 Squadron at Kenley, 1943.

Squadron Leader Hugh Godefroy DFC, commander of 403 Squadron who succeeded Johnnie Johnson as Kenley wing leader; he survived the war and later became a heart surgeon.

Group Captain 'Iron' Bill MacBrien, commanding 144 Wing on the continent after the invasion.

Flight Lieutenant Charlie Magwood, left, with an unidentified pilot at Kenley, 1943.

The Canadian Spitfire pilot Flying Officer Jackie Ray at Kenley in 1943, who returned to Canada after the war and became a well-known television presenter.

Flight Lieutenant Gordon Troke DFC, 443 Squadron, Kenley 1943.

A Canadian pilot who died whilst converting to Spitfires at 52 Operational Training Unit, Aston Down, near Stroud in Gloucestershire: Sergeant George Alvin Davis, a 21-year-old from Ontario. Whilst flying Spitfire P9546, the aircraft broke up in mid-air and crashed at Dymock, Gloucestershire, on 11 February 1942. This aircraft had been damaged in combat whilst on charge with 19 Squadron during the Battle of Britain, taking a round through the all-important mainspar, so it is possible that this contributed to the eventual structural failure.

Another Canadian who perished during training with 52 OTU was Sergeant Eldon Howard Caldwell of Alberta. On 26 January 1943, Caldwell was amongst pilots engaged on a gunnery practice sortie when his Spitfire, P8208, collided over the Severn Estuary with P8207, flown by Sergeant H. Clarke, the latter making a safe forced-landing on the foreshore at Magor. Sadly, Sergeant Caldwell crashed into the estuary and his remains were never found. The wreckage of his aircraft was recovered by this author and friends, working with an RAF team in 1993, and it is currently being restored to flying condition by Retro Track and Air at Dursley in Gloucestershire – within sight of the treacherous estuary.

Another Canadian answering the call was MacKenzie Reeves of Madoc, Ontario, who is pictured here shortly after receiving his coveted pilot's 'wings'. (*Brock Kerby*)

Later commissioned, Flying Officer MacKenzie Reeves flew Spitfires with 403 Squadron, one of fourteen RCAF fighter squadrons which flew during the Second World War, and was credited with four-and-a-half aerial victories before being killed in action on 28 March 1945. (*Brock Kerby*)

Above and following pages: Flying Officer Floyd Russell 'Bud' Loveless was another Canadian Spitfire pilot, surviving an incident during training when, on only his third flight in a Spitfire, only skilful flying saved both pilot and aircraft after an engine failure. He subsequently flew with 414 (RCAF) Squadron, and later photographic reconnaissance Spitfires, until shot down over Hamburg and captured on 24 April 1945 – fortunately, with the war ending just two weeks later, he was not in the 'bag' for long. (*Brock Kerby*)

Sergeant Peter Taylor, a Scot, was also trained overseas, joining 65 Squadron in 1943. From then onwards he was in action constantly, flying the usual round of offensive operations over France, including many bomber escort missions and dangerous ground-attack sorties. He is pictured here with a Spitfire Mk IX bearing a Canadian maple leaf insignia. Later commissioned, Peter also flew with 19 Squadron, which, along with 122 Squadron, was a part of 122 Wing with 65 Squadron, and also flew the Mustang III. He survived the war and retired to Worcester, where Peter died, aged 99, on 15 September 2022.

That universal fighter pilot language again: Peter Taylor listening to a colleague 'shooting a line'.

A great friend of Peter Taylor's was Tony Minchin, pictured here during training, who had a similar operational career, flying Spitfires and Mustangs with 122 Squadron.

A formal studio portrait of Pilot Officer Tony Minchin, whose story and diary extracts this author published in *A Few of the Many* (1995). A printer post-war, Tony retired to Malvern and met Peter Taylor again by chance at the launch of one of this author's books in 1992. The pair remained in close contact and were active members of their local Aircrew Association branch until Tony moved away to Dorset, where he died a few years ago.

64 Squadron's pilots crowding onto a jeep driven by an American at Kenley in 1943; the Rhodesian ace Johnny Plagis is standing holding a camera.

Brian Harris, from Droitwich, Worcestershire, joined 74 Squadron in 1942, with which he went out to North Africa. On 13 November 1943 the engine of his Spitfire, VS342, erupted into flame, causing Brian to crash-land, slightly injured. Back home, on 22 May 1944, he was flying Spitfire MK672 so low whilst strafing a German column near Ath in Belgium that he struck a tree, resulting in another forced landing. Captured, Brian was repatriated in 1945 and always recalled that 'Flying Spitfires is something that I am very proud of and was the most exciting time of my life'.

Sergeant Jack Allen trained at Bagotville, Canada, where he is pictured here in a Hurricane, and joined 616 Squadron at Exeter in the run-up to D-Day. He flew a number of offensive operations over France before being killed when 'beating up' his parents' farm near Leominster, Herefordshire, on 29 June 1944, in Spitfire Mk VII, MB762; he was 19.

Bob George was also a sergeant-pilot on 616 Squadron and recalled the tragedy well. In July 1944, 616 Squadron became the RAF's first jet fighter squadron, operating the Gloster Meteor, and Bob was amongst those first jet fighter boys.

Pilot Officer James Robert 'Jim Bob' Lee, from Comanche, Texas, was another American volunteer serving in the RAF. He was killed on 8 April 1942 whilst converting to Spitfires when his aircraft collided with a Wellington, also on a training flight, in challenging weather over Gloucestershire. Both aircraft crashed at Cold Aston, with all aircrew involved losing their lives. Jim Bob's grave can be found today in the picturesque churchyard at Little Rissington.

Opposite and below: Another American was Flying Officer Raimond Sanders Draper, who flew Spitfires from Hornchurch with 64 Squadron, where he is pictured here by Bob Poulton. On 24 March 1943, his Spitfire's engine failed almost immediately after take-off, on a trajectory towards Sutton School. Draper ensured that the aircraft crashed short of the buildings but was killed when the Spitfire turned over on impact. Today, the school is named in his honour.

All we know is that this Spitfire pilot, snapped by Bob Poulton, is one 'Flying Officer Patterson'. Uncaptioned photographs are the historian's perennial frustration, which becomes evident as this book continues.

64 Squadron's commander at Kenley in 1943 was a Belgian, Squadron Leader Michel 'Mike' Donet DFC; he survived the war.

Yet another American volunteer, also on 64 Squadron and snapped by Bob Poulton, was Flying Officer John Harder, a very experienced airman who spent a lifetime in aviation before his death in 1975.

Flying Officer Harder with the Polish Sergeant Remboski.

As these two pictures illustrate, animals were popular squadron mascots. Unfortunately, both of these Spitfire pilots, appearing in Bob Beardsley's, album, are unfortunately anonymous.

Typically anonymous groundcrew roughly applying D-Day stripes to a Spitfire prior to the invasion.

After D-Day the fighter squadrons led a nomadic existence, living in tented accommodation and keeping on the move, supporting the advancing Allied armies. Conditions were hard for the groundcrews, seen here maintaining a Spitfire on a temporary airstrip in Normandy.

After earlier operational tours, many fighter pilots ended up in training or other non-operational roles. A number clamoured for a return to 'ops' before it was all over, amongst them Battle of Britain veteran Flight Lieutenant Harry Welford (extreme right), who joined 222 Squadron to fly Spitfires at Wevelgem on 29 November 1944. Harry, whose story is included in this author's *Letters From The Few*, died in 1996.

John Slade came from Bristol and, after training, flew Spitfires with 237 'Rhodesia' Squadron during the Italian campaign and beyond. Heavily engaged with fighter-bomber missions, John survived being hit by flak but remained traumatised at seeing his friend's Spitfire explode in the air alongside him. He was reunited with a Spitfire by this author at Duxford, but sadly died soon afterwards after a long illness.

The next five photographs originate from Bob Beardsley's album and show pilots of 222 Squadron with Spitfire Mk IXs on the continent after D-Day. They are reproduced here with their original captions…
'Don't argue with the front end of a 190'.

'Dash and the secret weapon'.

'Big Aussie show off!'

Unfortunately there was no caption to this snapshot – who is he and what was the back story?

'Wacko, Bill and Dash'.

Whilst Group Captain Sir Douglas Bader's story remains well-known as the inspirational RAF fighter pilot with no legs, less so is the fact that although the first, he was not unique. This is Flight Lieutenant Colin Hodgkinson who lost both legs in a training accident but was still determined to fly Spitfires – which he did, scoring at least two victories before being captured on 24 November 1943, when forced to crash in France owing to oxygen failure. His memoir, *Best Foot Forward*, was published in 1957, a year after Paul Brickhill's best-selling Bader yarn *Reach for the Sky*, and remains a recommended read.

Having also been captured, in 1941, and repatriated in 1945, Group Captain Douglas Bader prepared to take-off from North Weald and lead the first post-war Battle of Britain Day flypast on 15 September 1945. Bader would later be knighted for services to the amputee community but died in 1982. Today, the Douglas Bader Foundation is a living memorial to him, continuing to support the amputee community in Sir Douglas's name.

Flight Lieutenant Maurice Macey first flew Spitfires in 1943 with 127 Squadron in Egypt. Returning home in April 1944, he joined 41 Squadron, flying Spitfire Mk IXs on dangerous low-level ground-attack sorties over France, and intercepting V-1 'Buzz Bombs'. On 14 August 1944, Maurice was hit by flak, crash-landing near Argentan, and was captured.

Flight Lieutenant Maurice Macey upon repatriation in 1945, having survived the infamous 'Death March', when the Germans marched prisoners west, away from the advancing Russians, in sub-zero conditions and with inadequate clothing, food or shelter; he was 22.

The Dutch Flying Officer Rudolph 'Rudi' Frans Burgwal, who flew Spitfires with 322 (Dutch) Squadron, becoming the eighteenth highest-scoring 'Diver' ace, having destroyed twenty-one of the V-1 flying bombs. On 13 August 1944, however, 322 Squadron, flying from the forward airfield at Deanland in Sussex, escorted Lancasters to bomb an ammunition dump near Orleans; over Le Genest-Saint Isle, Flying Officer Burgwal's Spitfire Mk IX, MH370, was hit by flak and crashed, killing the 26-year-old instantly. He was originally buried by the French in the Cemetery of the Commune St Isle, and after the war, when burials were concentrated by the IWGC (Imperial War Graves Commission), interred at Orry-la-Ville's 'Netherlands Field of Honour', where his grave can be found today.

Upon return from initial flying training in Rhodesia, Pilot Officer Ian Smith completed advanced service flying training at Ternhill, Shropshire, and was posted to RAF Station Petah Tiqva in Palestine for conversion to Spitfires. On the day of his death, Ian was flying Spitfire ER584, and crashed at 0957 hrs, 22 February 1945. On 27 February 1945, Ian's CO, Squadron Leader Sandeman, wrote to his father regarding the circumstances: 'Your son was posted to this unit to complete an operational training course before joining his squadron. He had been doing very well on the course, and his instructors had reported that he was making excellent progress. However, on 22 February 1945, he was carrying out a routine training flight away from the aerodrome when, during some manoeuvres, the aircraft became out of control and crashed, and your son was unfortunately killed instantaneously... Although Pilot Officer Smith was only here for a short while, it is felt that the RAF has lost an officer who it will be difficult to replace, and his loss will be deeply felt'.

'DCO': Duty Carried Out 2. Squadron Leader Laurence 'Rubber' Thorogood DFC, a Battle of Britain veteran, right, later commanded 273 Squadron in India, where he and colleagues are pictured in a Spitfire graveyard at the war's end. By that time, the Spitfire, thanks to those who designed, built, maintained and flew her, was an icon – and so it remains today. Most definitely a case of 'DCO'.

'DCO': Duty Carried Out 1. Whilst so many failed to return, and lie buried around the globe or simply missing, others returned from the war deeply scarred by their experiences. Sergeant F.E. Tullitt, pictured here, right, at an early post-war wedding, flew Spitfires with 54 Squadron at Hornchurch but was shot down over France, possibly by the German ace Egon Mayer, Staffelkapitän of 7/JG 2, on 12 July 1941, and baled out over Wormhoudt. Captured, the long years of captivity took their toll, and upon repatriation there was little or no help available for survivors. Sadly, Tullitt died in the late 1940s as a relatively young man.

Select Bibliography

Boot, H., & Sturtivant, R., *Gifts of War: Spitfires and other presentation aircraft in Two World Wars*, Air Britain (Historians) Ltd, Tonbridge, 2005

Mitchell, G., *R.J. Mitchell: World-Famous Aircraft Designer – Schooldays to Spitfires*, Nelson & Saunders Publishers, Olney, 1986

Morgan, E., & Shacklady, E., *Spitfire: The History*, Key Publishing, Stamford, 1987

Price, A, *The Spitfire Story*, Arms & Armour Press Ltd, London, 1986

Russell, CR, *Spitfire Odyssey: My Life at Supermarines 1936-1957*, Kingfisher Railway Productions, Southampton, 1985

Shores, C., & Williams, C., *Aces High*, Grub Street, London, 1994

Wynn, K.G., *Men of the Battle of Britain*, Frontline Books/Pen & Sword, Barnsley, 2015

Anyone wishing to know more about the 'Supermariners', the men and women responsible for creating and building the Spitfire in and around Southampton, can do no better than to look up Dave Key's informative website: https://supermariners.wordpress.com

Acknowledgements

Always grateful to the numerous friends, most sadly now deceased, who have donated photographs to the archive over the last forty years.

Very grateful to my friend and publisher Martin Mace for his ongoing support, and in this case organising the scanning for this book, and as always, the Pen & Sword team were a pleasure to work with.

Other Books by Dilip Sarkar